DATE DUE   7/10/00

WILDLIFE OF NORTH AMERICA

The Polar Bear

by Annie Hemstock

Consultant:
Steven C. Amstrup, Ph.D.
Polar Bear Project Leader
USGS Alaska Biological Science Center

CAPSTONE
HIGH/LOW BOOKS
an imprint of Capstone Press
Mankato, Minnesota

Capstone High/Low Books are published by Capstone Press
818 North Willow Street • Mankato, Minnesota 56001
http://www.capstone-press.com

Library of Congress Cataloging-in-Publication Data
Hemstock, Annie.
    The polar bear/by Annie Hemstock.
    p. cm.—(Wildlife of North America)
    Includes bibliographical references (p. 45) and index.
    Summary: Describes the physical characteristics, life cycle, relations with
humans, and survival methods of the world's largest land carnivore.
    ISBN 0-7368-0031-X
    1. Polar bear—Juvenile literature. [1. Polar bear. 2. Bears.] I. Title.
II. Series.
    QL737.C27H46 1999
    599.786—dc21

                                                                    98-3482
                                                                       CIP
                                                                        AC

Editorial Credits

Mark Drew, editor; Timothy Halldin, cover designer and illustrator;
    Sheri Gosewisch, photo researcher

Photo Credits

Dan Guravich, 20, 30
Dembinsky Photo Assoc. Inc./Claudia Adams, 33; Fritz Polking, 34
Leonard Lee Rue, 19
Marcia M. Guravich, 12, 26
Michele Burgess, 18
Photo Network/Mark Newman, cover, 10; Howard Folsom, 15, 28
Photophile/Lindsey Martin, 6, 38, 41
Ronald Cantor, 23
Root Resources/Claudia Adams, 43
Valan Photos/Fred Bruemmer, 25
The Wildlife Collection/Gary Schultz, 16; Robert Larkinen, 36–37

Table of Contents

Fast Facts about Polar Bears

Scientific Name: *Ursus maritimus*

Length: Adult male polar bears are eight to 10 feet (2.4 to three meters) long from nose to tail. Adult females are six to eight feet (1.8 to 2.4 meters) long.

Weight: Adult male polar bears weigh from 775 pounds (352 kilograms) to more than 1,500 pounds (680 kilograms). Adult female bears usually weigh from 330 to 550 pounds (150 to 249 kilograms). Females can weigh as much as 1,100 pounds (499 kilograms) before giving birth.

Physical Features: Polar bears have heavy bodies, strong legs, and sharp teeth. Their heads and ears are small compared to those of brown bears. Polar bears' necks are longer than the necks of other bears.

Color: Polar bears' coats appear white or cream colored. But their fur is actually clear. Polar bears sometimes look brown or yellow when their fur becomes dirty or stained. Polar bears' skin, noses, and claws are black.

Range: Polar bears live in the Arctic regions of Canada and Alaska. They also live in the Arctic areas of Greenland, Norway, and Russia.

Habitat: Polar bears live on the ice that covers much of the Arctic Ocean. They sometimes live on Arctic coasts.

Behavior: Adult polar bears live alone most of their lives. They are active all year. They hunt both day and night.

Food: Polar bears mostly eat seals. They sometimes eat walruses and beluga whales. Polar bears also eat fish, birds, plants, and garbage if these are available.

Reproduction: Polar bears mate on the Arctic ice during April and May. Cubs are usually born between November and January.

Life Span: Polar bears can live up to 30 years.

Chapter 1

The Polar Bear

Polar bears are the largest members of the bear family. All members of the bear family are mammals. A mammal is a warm-blooded animal with a backbone. The body temperature of a warm-blooded animal stays about the same despite the air temperature. Polar bears also are carnivores. Most of the polar bear's diet consists of meat.

Eight species of bears live in the world today. A species is a group of animals with similar features. Members of a species can mate and produce young. Polar bears are one of three species of bears that live in North America. The other two species are brown bears and North

Polar bears are the largest members of the bear family.

7

American black bears. Polar bears are most closely related to brown bears.

Range and Habitat

Polar bears live in the Arctic regions of Alaska, Canada, Greenland, Norway, and Russia. The Arctic is the area that surrounds the North Pole. It includes the Arctic Ocean and the northern parts of North America, Europe, and Asia. Scientists named polar bears after the North Pole.

Huge sheets of ice cover much of the Arctic all year. These ice sheets become larger during winter as more water freezes. They thaw and shrink during summer. Some Arctic ice connects to land. Other Arctic ice forms into floes that drift with the currents of Arctic waters.

Polar bears live mainly on Arctic ice. They try to remain close to the southern edge of the ice. The ice constantly freezes, thaws, and cracks there. This causes areas of open water called leads to form in the ice. Seals often gather near leads. Seals are the main source of food for polar bears.

Where Polar Bears Live

Polar bears try to stay on the ice all year. It is easier for them to hunt from ice than from water or land. Polar bears are forced to live on land in areas where the ice completely melts during summer.

Polar bears have small ears and sharp teeth.

Physical Features
Polar bears have heavy bodies, strong legs, and sharp teeth. They also have long necks, small ears, and short tails.

Polar bears' coats appear white or cream colored. But their fur is actually clear. Their coats act as camouflage when polar bears hunt. The light color of polar bears' coats helps the bears blend in with snow and ice.

Polar bears have black skin under their thick coats. Some scientists believe black skin helps the bears collect and store heat. Polar bears also have black noses, lips, and tongues.

Size

Adult male polar bears weigh from 775 pounds (352 kilograms) to more than 1,500 pounds (680 kilograms). They are eight to 10 feet (2.4 to three meters) long from nose to tail. The largest polar bear on record was a male that measured 12 feet (3.7 meters) long. He weighed 2,209 pounds (1,002 kilograms).

Adult female polar bears usually are much smaller than males. Females weigh from 330 to 550 pounds (150 to 249 kilograms). They can weigh up to 1,100 pounds (499 kilograms) before giving birth. Female polar bears are about six to eight feet (1.8 to 2.4 meters) long.

Polar bears sleep in many different positions.

Behavior

Polar bears are active all year. They spend much of their time searching for seals and other prey. They do not sleep through the winter like other bears. Polar bears are most active during winter.

Polar bears often sleep after meals. They sleep in many different places and positions. Polar bears often just curl up and cover their noses to sleep on Arctic ice. They sometimes sleep in pits they have dug in snow drifts. Pits shelter polar bears from cold winds.

Adult polar bears live alone most of their lives. But during mating season, male and female bears travel together. Cubs stay with their mothers for about two and one-half years. A cub is a young polar bear.

Polar bears sometimes meet on the ice near good hunting sites. They also gather on land during summer and fall in places where the ice completely melts. The bears play-fight, chase each other, and sleep while they wait for the ice to return.

Communication

Polar bears communicate through the sounds they make. They growl, hiss, and gnash their teeth when they are upset. Cubs cry, smack their lips, and growl. Female polar bears grunt to warn their cubs of danger.

Polar bears also use their bodies to communicate. They can tell if other polar bears are dangerous by the way these bears approach. Polar bears with their heads lowered and ears flattened are angry or upset. Bears with their heads lowered, mouths closed, and eyes looking away are not dangerous.

Mother polar bears use their bodies to communicate with their cubs. They often nuzzle their cubs with their snouts to comfort them. A polar bear's snout is the front part of its face. It includes the polar bear's nose, mouth, and jaw.

Home Range

Each polar bear lives in an area called a home range. The size of a home range is different for each bear. Some polar bears have home ranges of more than 200,000 square miles (518,000 square kilometers).

Many factors affect the size of polar bears' home ranges. The movements of seal populations can affect home range size. Polar bears must find the seals when seals move to new places.

The way Arctic ice freezes, thaws, and breaks up also affects home range size. Home ranges may be small if they include many leads and seals. If not, polar bears must increase their home ranges to find leads and seals.

Mother polar bears often use their snouts to comfort their cubs.

Polar bears are not territorial. They do not protect their home ranges from other polar bears. They often meet other polar bears in places where seals are plentiful. Polar bears will fight to protect prey they have caught.

Chapter 2

Survival

The polar bear's habitat always changes. Ice freezes, breaks, and thaws throughout the year. Polar bears must adapt to these changes. Seals also move from place to place as the ice changes. Polar bears must try to follow seals in order to survive.

The climate of the Arctic can be rough. Strong freezing winds blow across the Arctic ice. Winters are long and cold. Summers are short and cool. Snowstorms often occur during summer and fall. Polar bears have many qualities that help them survive in this harsh climate.

Polar bears have many qualities that help them survive in the rough climate of the Arctic.

The polar bear's feet help it travel on ice.

Keeping Warm

A thick layer of fat called blubber keeps polar
bears warm. Polar bears depend on blubber to
keep them alive. Their bodies use blubber for
energy when food is scarce. Polar bears need

energy to produce body heat. Blubber also helps polar bears stay afloat when they swim.

Polar bears have heavy coats to keep them warm. Their winter coats are thicker than their summer coats. Polar bears' coats can be up to two inches (5.1 centimeters) thick.

Polar bears' coats have two layers of hair. The bottom layer is woolly fur. This fur helps keep body heat from escaping. A layer of shiny guard hair protects the woolly fur.

Traveling over Ice and Snow

Polar bears often walk great distances to find seals or other prey. The polar bear's feet help it travel on ice.

Polar bears' feet can be up to 12 inches (31 centimeters) wide. The size of their feet helps

POLAR BEAR TRACKS

Front Track   Back Track

polar bears walk over thin ice. Large feet spread out polar bears' weight. This often helps to keep the ice from breaking. Polar bears crawl on their bellies if the ice is very thin. This helps spread out their weight even more.

Polar bears have thick, curved claws. These claws keep them from slipping on ice and snow. Claws also help polar bears catch and hold onto prey. Polar bear claws can be more than two inches (5.1 centimeters) long.

Polar bears have black pads on the bottoms of their feet. Small, soft bumps called papillae (puh-PIL-eye) cover these footpads. The papillae grip the ice to keep polar bears from slipping as they walk. Fur that grows between polar bears' toes and pads also prevents slipping.

Polar Bears in Water

Polar bears often swim between ice floes in their search for prey. Their large feet work like paddles. Polar bears are strong

Polar bears often swim between ice floes in their search for prey.

swimmers. They can swim more than three miles (4.8 kilometers) per hour for long distances. Scientists have seen polar bears swim more than 60 miles (97 kilometers) without stopping.

Polar bears sometimes dive below the water's surface when looking for food or swimming between floes. They can stay underwater for up to three minutes.

Natural oils in polar bears' coats help them dry off after a swim. The oils cover polar bears' fur. Polar bears shake themselves when they come out of the water. Most of the water shakes out easily because of the oils.

Food

The polar bear's diet consists mostly of seals. Seals have large amounts of blubber. This blubber is a rich food source for the polar bear.

Seals spend much of their time swimming underneath the ice. But they must come up for air. Seals come up to the surface near the edges of Arctic ice. They also make holes in

Seals sometimes leave the water to rest on the ice.

the ice so they can come up to breathe. Seals
sometimes leave the water to rest on the ice.

Polar bears use their sense of smell to locate
seals. They can detect the scent of seals
through more than three feet (one meter) of
snow. Polar bears also can smell seals and

other food that is 20 miles (32 kilometers) away from them.

Polar bears must find other food when they cannot find seals. Polar bears will eat dead seals, walruses, and whales that wash up on shore. They will eat reindeer, fish, and sea birds if these animals are available. They sometimes eat plants, berries, and birds' eggs.

Some polar bears eat human garbage when other food is not available. Young polar bears and females with cubs are most likely to raid garbage dumps.

Hunting Methods

Polar bears use several methods to hunt seals. Scientists call the most common method still-hunting.

A polar bear waits on the edge of the ice or near a seal's breathing hole when still-hunting. It waits for a seal to come to the surface. A polar bear sometimes must wait more than a day. The bear usually lies on its stomach while it waits. It stays very still and quiet because seals frighten easily. The polar bear

A polar bear waits on the edge of the ice when still-hunting.

Polar bears eat seal skin and blubber first because they provide the most energy.

then grabs a seal when it surfaces and pulls it from the water.

Polar bears also use the stalking method to catch seals. The bears stalk seals that are resting on the ice.

A polar bear using the stalking method will stand very still when it spots a seal. The bear then creeps slowly over the snow and ice. It does this until it gets within 50 to 100 feet (15 to 30 meters) of its prey. The polar bear then charges at the seal and tries to catch it.

In the spring, female seals build caves under snow that has drifted over their breathing holes. They give birth to their pups in these caves. Polar bears sometimes raid seal caves. Mother seals and their pups have large amounts of blubber. To catch seals in caves, polar bears stand on their hind legs. They then smash through the caves' roofs with their front legs.

Adult polar bears usually eat only the skin and blubber of seals. Skin and blubber provide bears with the most energy. Polar bears frequently leave seal flesh behind. Arctic foxes, seagulls, and young polar bears eat the flesh.

Chapter 3

Life Cycle

Polar bears mate on Arctic ice during April and May. Females mate for the first time at about four years old. Males mate for the first time between the ages of eight and 10.

Polar bears find each other by gathering where the seal hunting is best. Males also track females that are ready to mate. A male will follow a female's tracks for as long as it takes to find her.

Male polar bears often fight other males for females. Males attack with heads lowered, ears flattened, and mouths open. They make a hissing roar. Male bears sometimes stand on

Male polar bears often fight one another for females.

Female polar bears often dig their dens in snowbanks on hillsides.

their hind legs and face each other. They then try to push each other over.

Male polar bears may injure each other while fighting. But the fights usually are not deadly. The bigger, stronger male chases the other male away. The winner stays with the female bear for a week or more. Then he leaves her to mate with other females.

Female polar bears gain weight after they have mated. They may double their weight before their cubs are born. Female bears often feed on female seals and pups to put on weight. These are easy prey for female polar bears to catch.

Digging Dens

Female bears that have mated look for places to dig dens in October and November. Dens usually are on land within 10 miles (16 kilometers) of the water. Females often dig their dens in snowbanks on hillsides. Some females dig dens in the snowdrifts that form on the ice.

Female bears stay in their dens for long periods of

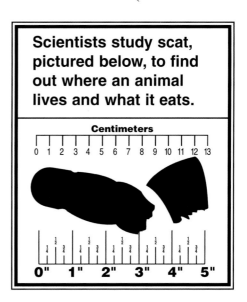

Scientists study scat, pictured below, to find out where an animal lives and what it eats.

time. Some females stay in their dens for up to nine months. They do not eat while in their dens. Female bears spend most of that time sleeping in their dens.

Cubs are born in the dens sometime between November and January. Most female polar bears have two cubs. Cubs weigh just 16 to 24 ounces (454 to 680 grams) at birth. They are only about 12 inches (30 centimeters) long.

Newborn cubs are helpless. Their eyes stay closed for about a month. Cubs are not born with thick coats. The heat from their mother's body protects them from the cold.

Growing Up

Polar bear cubs spend their first few weeks of life nursing. The mother bear's rich milk helps her cubs grow quickly. Cubs start walking when they are about two months old.

The mother bear leads her cubs out of the den in March or April. Winter snows sometimes cover the den's original entrance. The mother may have to dig a way out.

A polar bear family stays near its den for about two weeks while the cubs become used to the cold.

The family stays near the den for about two weeks while the cubs become used to the cold. The cubs practice walking on snow and ice. They chase each other and play-fight. Cubs sleep in the den at night. The mother bear takes her cubs onto the ice when they are big enough to travel.

The cubs start eating solid food soon after they leave the den. At first, the mother hunts for food while the cubs watch. This is how the cubs learn to hunt. Cubs kill their own prey when they are about one year old.

The mother polar bear protects her cubs. She will fight to the death to defend them from predators such as wolves. Predators hunt and eat other animals.

The cubs stay with their mother until they are about two and one-half years old. Then the mother often chases them away. Males interested in mating also chase the cubs away. The mother bear is then ready to mate again.

Many young polar bears die in the first few years after they leave their mothers. Some cannot find enough food to survive. Predators kill other young bears. Only the strongest and luckiest polar bears survive into adulthood. Polar bears become adults at about five years old.

Few polar bears live to be more than 25 years old. The oldest wild polar bear on record was 32 years old. One polar bear in a zoo lived to be 41.

Cubs stay with their mothers until they are about two and one-half years old.

Small Ears

Snout

Strong Legs

Chapter 4

Past and Future

Scientists believe the first polar bears appeared about 250,000 years ago. They think that brown bears living near the Arctic slowly adapted to their surroundings. Their hair became thicker and heavier to protect them from the cold. Their coats became lighter in color to help them blend in with snow and ice.

Scientists say the process of adapting to the Arctic took thousands of years. Eventually, these Arctic brown bears separated from other brown bears. They then became polar bears.

Scientists believe the first polar bears appeared about 250,000 years ago.

Polar Bears and People

Polar bears have helped native peoples survive in the Arctic. Native peoples have hunted polar bears for thousands of years. Polar bears provided them with food, clothing, and bedding.

Native peoples have always had great respect for polar bears. Some native peoples believed the bears let hunters kill them. They thought that a dead polar bear's spirit would visit living bears. The spirit would tell other bears how people had treated it. Other bears would not let hunters kill them if the hunters had mistreated the dead bear.

During the 900s, European explorers entered the Arctic for the first time. More and more explorers ventured into the Arctic as years passed. Many of these people did not treat polar bears with respect. Explorers hunted polar bears mostly for sport and for their hides.

People began using airplanes and motorboats to hunt polar bears in the 1950s. Airplanes and motorboats made it easier to catch and kill polar bears. The polar bear

Polar bears became a threatened species in 1975.

population decreased because people killed too many bears. The polar bear became a threatened species in 1975. Polar bears were in danger of dying out.

The five countries where polar bears live made an agreement in 1976. They would not allow people to hunt polar bears from airplanes or large motorboats.

Polar Bears Today

Today, fewer people may hunt polar bears. The polar bear population has increased because of the 1976 agreement. The polar bear population is now between 20,000 and 40,000. Native peoples who depend on polar bears for survival may still hunt them.

Today, polar bears face new threats from humans. People drilling for oil or gas may disturb female bears in their dens. Oil spills and toxic chemicals could pollute Arctic waters and polar bears' home ranges.

Scientists are working to understand more about the polar bear and its Arctic habitat. They are learning more about the ways that humans affect polar bears and their surroundings. Scientists are using what they learn to protect the polar bear's future.

Many ordinary people also are interested in polar bears. Books, photographs, and films about polar bears are very popular. Thousands of people crowd the town of Churchill, Manitoba, each fall to watch the

Thousands of people crowd the town of Churchill, Manitoba, each fall to watch the polar bears.

polar bears. The bears gather there during summer to wait for the ice to return to Hudson Bay. People's interest in polar bears will help make sure these animals continue to survive.

Words to Know

blubber (BLUH-bur)—the layer of fat under the skin of the polar bear, whale, and seal
camouflage (KAM-uh-flahzh)—coloring that makes something look like its surroundings
carnivore (KAR-nuh-vor)—an animal that eats meat
communicate (kuh-MYOO-nuh-kate)—to send and receive messages
floe (FLOH)—a large sheet of floating ice
hibernate (HYE-bur-nate)—to spend the winter in a deep sleep
mammal (MAM-uhl)—a warm-blooded animal with a backbone
papillae (puh-PIL-eye)—small, soft bumps that cover a polar bear's footpads
predator (PRED-uh-tur)—an animal that hunts and eats other animals
species (SPEE-sheez)—a group of animals with similar features; members of a species can mate and produce young.
threatened (THRET-uhnd)—in danger of dying out

44

To Learn More

Buff, Sheila. *Bears*. Nature's Window. Kansas City, Mo.: Andrews and McMeel, 1997.

Gilks, Helen. *Bears*. New York: Ticknor & Fields, 1993.

Hodge, Deborah. *Bears: Polar Bears, Black Bears, Grizzly Bears*. Toronto: Kids Can Press, 1997.

Matthews, Downs. *Polar Bear Cubs*. New York: Simon and Schuster Books for Young Readers, 1989.

Stirling, Ian. *Bears*. Sierra Club Wildlife Library. San Francisco: Sierra Club Books for Children, 1992.

Useful Addresses

Alaska Department of Fish and Game
P.O. Box 25526
Juneau, AK 99802-5526

Arctic National Wildlife Refuge
101 12th Avenue
Box 20
Fairbanks, AK 99701

Churchill Northern Studies Centre
P.O. Box 610
Churchill, Manitoba R0B 0E0
Canada

National Wildlife Federation
8925 Leesburg Pike
Vienna, VA 22184

Internet Sites

ADF&G's Wildlife Notebook Series: Polar Bear
http://www.state.ak.us/local/akpages/FISH.GAME/
   notebook/marine/polarbea.htm

The Bear Den—Polar Bears
http://www.nature-net.com/bears/polar.html

Polar Bear
http://www.pbs.org/kratts/world/na/polar/
   index.html

USGS Biological Resources: Polar Bear
http://biology.usgs.gov/features/kidscorner/
   polarb.html

Index

Alaska, 5, 8
Arctic, 5, 8, 17, 39, 40
Arctic Ocean, 5, 8

behavior, 5, 12–13
blubber, 18, 19, 22, 27
breathing hole, 24, 27

camouflage, 11
Canada, 5, 8
Churchill, Manitoba, 42
claws, 4, 21
coat, 4, 11, 19, 22, 32, 39
communication, 13–14
cub, 5, 13, 14, 24, 31, 32, 33, 35

den, 31, 32, 33, 35

floes, 8, 21, 22
food, 5, 8, 18, 22–24, 35, 40
fur, 4, 11, 19, 21, 22

habitat, 5, 8–9, 17, 42
home range, 14–15, 42
hunting 24–27, 29

leads, 8, 14

native peoples, 40, 42
North America, 7, 8

papillae, 21
predator, 35
prey, 12, 15, 19, 21, 35
pups, 27, 31

range, 5, 8–9

seal, 5, 8, 12, 14, 15, 17, 19, 22, 23, 24, 26, 27, 31
size, 11, 14, 19
species, 7, 41
stalking method, 26, 27
still-hunting, 24